Sports Illustrated KIDS
SOCCER RECORDS SMASHED!

by Brendan Flynn

CAPSTONE PRESS
a capstone imprint

Published by Capstone Press, an imprint of Capstone
1710 Roe Crest Drive, North Mankato, Minnesota 56003
capstonepub.com

SPORTS ILLUSTRATED KIDS is a trademark of ABG-SI LLC. Used with permission.

Library of Congress Cataloging-in-Publication Data
Names: Flynn, Brendan, author.
Title: Soccer records smashed! / by Brendan Flynn.
Description: North Mankato, Minnesota : Capstone Press, [2024] | Series: Sports Illustrated kids. Record smashers | Includes bibliographical references and index. | Audience: Ages 9–11 | Audience: Grades 4–6 | Summary: "In soccer, fast footwork can lead to some fantastic feats—like Carli Lloyd's early hat trick during a 2015 Women's World Cup match and Miroslav Klose breaking Ronaldo's record for the most World Cup goals. In this Sports Illustrated Kids book, young readers can experience record-breaking plays in soccer. Fast-paced and fact-filled, this collection of record smashers will delight sports fans with thrilling achievements in soccer history"—Provided by publisher.
Identifiers: LCCN 2023003514 (print) | LCCN 2023003515 (ebook) | ISBN 9781669050179 (hardcover) | ISBN 9781669071617 (paperback) | ISBN 9781669050131 (pdf) | ISBN 9781669050155 (kindle edition) | ISBN 9781669050162 (epub)
Subjects: LCSH: Soccer—Records—Juvenile literature. | Soccer—History—Juvenile literature.
Classification: LCC GV943.25 .F648 2024 (print) | LCC GV943.25 (ebook) | DDC 796.334—dc23/eng/20230209
LC record available at https://lccn.loc.gov/2023003514
LC ebook record available at https://lccn.loc.gov/2023003515

Editorial Credits
Editor: Ericka Smith; Designer: Terri Poburka; Media Researcher: Svetlana Zhurkin; Production Specialist: Katy LaVigne

Image Credits
Associated Press: File/Elaine Thompson, cover (front), Joel Martinez, 21, The Canadian Press/Darryl Dyck, 6; Getty Images: Al Bello, 18, Alex Caparros, 11, Alexander Hassenstein, 10, Alexandre Schneider, 19, Bongart/Dennis Grombkowski, 9, David Ramos, 12, 13, Dennis Grombkowski, 7, FIFA/Stuart Franklin, 8, Kevin C. Cox, 4, 23, Laurence Griffiths, 26, Michael Steele, 22, 25, Robert Cianflone, 27, 29, Shaun Clark, 15, 16, Victor Fraile, 5; Newscom: Icon Sportswire/Ric Tapia, 20, Polaris/isiphotos/Ben Queenborough, 28, Zuma Press/PI/Javier Rojas, 14, 17; Shutterstock: Igor Link, cover (soccer ball), irin-k, cover (back), krissikunterbunt (fireworks), cover and throughout, pixssa (cracked background), 1 and throughout

All internet sites appearing in back matter were available and accurate when this book was sent to press.

TABLE OF CONTENTS

Words in **bold** are in the glossary.

GET YOUR KICKS!

Soccer is an old game. It started in England in the 1800s. Over the years, players have set some incredible records.

LLOYD LIFTS USA

In the finals of the 2015 Women's World Cup (WWC), the United States faced Japan. Early in the game, U.S. star Carli Lloyd had the ball near midfield. Japan's goalkeeper was out of position. So Lloyd sent a long kick toward the net.

Carli Lloyd

The goalkeeper scrambled back. But she couldn't reach it. Lloyd scored!

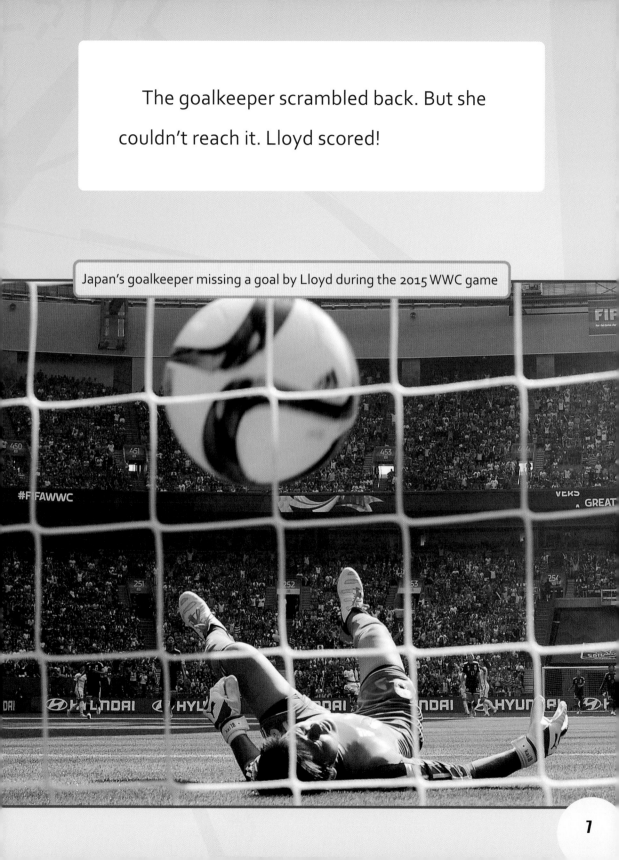

Japan's goalkeeper missing a goal by Lloyd during the 2015 WWC game

Lloyd celebrating her goal

Most players are happy to score once in a game. This was Lloyd's third goal! And the match was only 16 minutes old.

No player had ever scored a **hat trick** that early in a WWC match. Earlier in the tournament, Germany's Célia Šašić had set a record by completing a hat trick 31 minutes into a match.

Šašić scoring a hat trick during a 2015 WWC game

MAGNIFICENT MESSI

Lionel Messi is one of the greatest soccer players in history. The forward from Argentina **dribbles** through crowds. He passes to his teammates for wide-open shots. And he scores goals at a record pace.

Lionel Messi (center)

In a game on December 9, 2012, Messi blasted a shot past the goalkeeper. He smashed the record for most goals in a **calendar year**. Gerd Müller had set the previous record of 85 goals in 1972.

Messi had a few more games that year. He ended 2012 with 91 goals.

Messi played for two teams in 2012—FC Barcelona and Argentina's national team. He scored 79 goals for FC Barcelona and 12 for Argentina that year.

Messi (10) celebrating his new record with his teammates

LET'S GO, VELA!

In 2019, Carlos Vela had his eyes on a big record. The Los Angeles Football Club (LAFC) striker was piling up goals. On October 6, he made history.

Carlos Vela (center)

During a game, Vela gathered a pass near the **penalty area**. He had his back to the net. He spun to his right and tapped the ball with his left foot. Then, he launched a shot into the net.

Vela celebrating his first goal during the game on October 6, 2019

Vela's teammates mobbed him. The crowd cheered. That was his 32nd goal of the season. No player in Major League Soccer (MLS) had scored more in one season. Later in the game, Vela scored two more goals. His record of 34 goals will be tough to break.

Vela kicking his second goal during the game on October 6, 2019

CAPTAIN CHRISTINE

When Abby Wambach retired in 2015, she had scored 184 goals. That seemed like a record no one would top. But Christine Sinclair had other ideas.

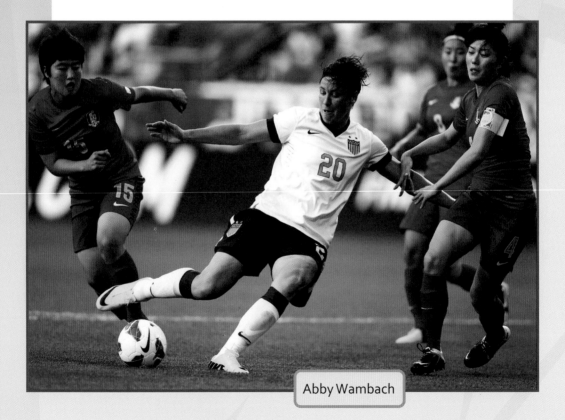

Abby Wambach

Christine Sinclair

Sinclair is an outstanding scorer. She scored her first goal for Canada in 2000. Twenty years later, she was still going strong. On January 29, 2020, Sinclair scored her 185th career goal. She smashed Wambach's record!

Sinclair led Canada to its first Olympic
gold medal in soccer in 2021.

HOWARD'S BIG DAY

During the 2014 World Cup, goalkeeper Tim Howard had his hands full. The U.S. had reached the **knockout** stage. In the Round of 16, they faced a tough Belgian team.

Over and over, the Belgians attacked. But Howard stood tall in the goal.

Howard making a save during the 2014 World Cup game

The U.S. defenders were outmatched. But Howard kept frustrating Belgium with amazing saves.

In the end, Belgium won. But Howard smashed a record. He'd made 16 saves. That was more saves than anyone had made in a single World Cup match. The old record was 13 saves. Peru's Ramón Quiroga set that record in 1978.

FACT

Howard also played for Manchester United and Everton in England's Premier League.

KLOSE TAKES THE CROWN

During the 2014 World Cup semifinal, Germany upset Brazil with a 7–1 win. It was a shocking defeat for Brazil. One of Germany's seven goals was especially important. An early goal by Miroslav Klose set a new record.

The 2014 World Cup semifinal game

Klose taking a shot during the 2014 World Cup semifinal game

In the first half of the game, Klose scored off a **rebound** of his own shot. That goal was his 16th career World Cup goal. He smashed the old record of 15 goals set by Brazil's Ronaldo in 2006!

Klose celebrating his record-breaking goal

FACT

Klose played in four World Cups. He scored his first three goals in a game against Saudi Arabia in 2002.

GLOSSARY

calendar year (KAL-uhn-duhr YEER)—from January 1 to December 31 of a year

dribble (DRI-buhl)—to move the ball along by kicking it with your feet

hat trick (HAT TRIK)—when a player scores three goals in one game

knockout (NOK-out)—a part of a tournament in which one loss removes a team from the competition

penalty area (PEN-uhl-tee AIR-ee-uh)—the bigger box in front of the goal on a soccer field; if the defense commits a foul in that area, the other team is awarded a penalty kick

rebound (REE-bound)—when the ball bounces off the goalkeeper or the goalpost

READ MORE

Berglund, Bruce. *Football Records Smashed!*
North Mankato, MN: Capstone, 2024.

Leed, Percy. *Abby Wambach: Super Striker.* Minneapolis:
Lerner, 2023.

Mattern, Joanne. *Trailblazing Women in Soccer.* Chicago:
Norwood House, 2023.

INTERNET SITES

FIFA: Women's World Cup
fifa.com/tournaments/womens/womensworldcup

Football Reference: Football Statistics and History
fbref.com/en

Major League Soccer
mlssoccer.com

INDEX

ABOUT THE AUTHOR

Brendan Flynn is a San Francisco resident and an author of numerous children's books. In addition to writing about sports, Flynn also enjoys competing in triathlons, Scrabble tournaments, and chili cook-offs.